WΦW

Choosing
a Career in
Real Estate

A real estate agent must be excellent at working with clients.

Choosing a Career in Real Estate

Betty Clark

The Rosen Publishing Group, Inc.
New York

To my daughter Patty, Realtor extraordinaire.

Published in 2001 by The Rosen Publishing Group, Inc.
29 East 21st Street, New York, NY 10010

Copyright © 2001 by The Rosen Publishing Group, Inc.

First Edition

Library of Congress Cataloging-in-Publication Data

Clark, Betty (Betty L.)
  Choosing a career in real estate / by Betty Clark. — 1st ed.
        p. cm. — (World of work)
Includes bibliographical references and index.
Summary: Describes a career as a real estate agent and the classes, activities, and other preparations necessary to be successful in this field.
  ISBN: 978-1-4358-8665-0
  1. Real estate business—Vocational guidance—Juvenile literature. 2. Real estate agents—Juvenile literature [1. Real estate business—Vocational guidance 2. Vocational guidance.] I. Title II. World of work (New York, N.Y.)
   HD1375 .C586 2000
   333.33'023'73—dc21
                                        00-008883

Manufactured in the United States of America

Contents

Introduction: Is a Real Estate Career
    for You?   6

1   What Does It Take to Enter the Field?   9

2   Pre-Licensing Activities   14

3   Finding the Right Broker   22

4   Responsibilities and Duties   33

5   Related Careers   48

Glossary   56

For More Information   59

For Further Reading   61

Index   62

Introduction:
Is a Real Estate
Career for You?

Selling homes, listing properties for sale, knowing the probable value of land, businesses, and homes—does that sound like an interesting career for you? If so, you may want to consider a career in real estate.

Today, some people in the field of real estate can make a fantastic amount of money just by listing a house (getting the right to sell it), showing a home, and selling a piece of property. Simple? Maybe—and maybe not. Maybe you would find it stressful, frightening, and hardly worth the effort.

There are many questions to think about as you consider entering the real estate field. Just how difficult is it to become a real estate agent? How does one go about it? How much does it cost? What training, skills, and talents are necessary to become a successful real estate salesperson?

Are there required classes? Are there many tests? Is there an apprenticeship program or on-the-job training? Is a college degree necessary, and how long would it take to get licensed to sell real estate in your hometown? How much money can

Working in the field of real estate can be exciting and financially rewarding.

a person expect to make? Can a beginner survive? How soon does one get a paycheck?

These are all questions that one should ask as he or she ventures into the world of work—whether in real estate or any other career. Certainly one thing is clear: You are already on the right track. You are taking steps to learn about a career. You are seeking facts, reading up on the pros and cons—the advantages and disadvantages—of making real estate your chosen field.

There are many benefits to working in real estate. It can be an exciting and rewarding career, and it can be quite profitable if you are willing to put in the effort. You can be your own boss and manage your own time. In addition, real estate is a field in which you can invest a minimal amount of tuition, yet gain the potential to earn as much as people in professions that require many years of college and graduate study. Read on to find out some of the answers to your questions and to learn more about the field of real estate.

1

What Does It Take to Enter the Field?

Of course, success won't happen overnight. There are few careers that produce overnight wonders. In almost any job, it is necessary to work hard, develop specific skills, and do research and planning on your own to make success happen.

Getting Advice

One very helpful tactic is to talk to employed adults to find out how they feel about their profession. How would they change their working lives if they could? Did they happen to drift into a certain field or did they choose a career very early? How do they feel about their job now?

As you consider real estate as a career for you, talking to people in real estate about their jobs is especially helpful. Talk to people who are doing what you think you might be doing a few months or a year from now.

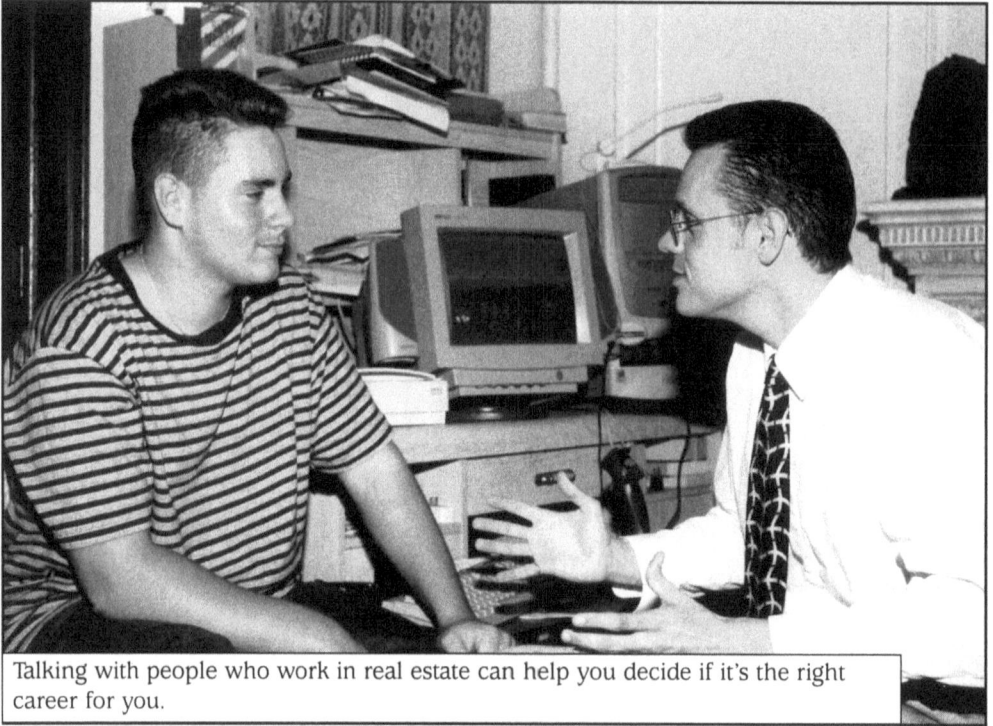

Talking with people who work in real estate can help you decide if it's the right career for you.

People Skills

One important skill that these people will tell you about is dealing with the public. You have to like people, enjoy helping them solve their problems, answer their questions, listen to them, and put up with a wide variety of personalities. If you have ever had any kind of "people job" before, you already understand the importance of being agreeable no matter how outlandishly the client behaves. You must be tolerant and patient.

If you are willing to learn a little each day, study until you get your license, know your product (properties), listen to the needs of your clients, serve them in a trustworthy manner, and learn to use up-to-date tools of the trade, there is good reason to believe that you can reach the top of the field.

Training

Getting into real estate doesn't have to be difficult. The investment in your own future will be small compared to what is required for most professional occupations. You could start today by finding out how to get licensed in your state. If you are still in school, a job or career counselor can help you find the necessary telephone numbers or addresses.

There are classes designed for people who have full-time jobs. If money is a problem, there are grants and agencies that may be able to support you as you seek a professional career to better your situation. Don't be discouraged. Stay with it if you are determined to go into real estate.

The required real estate classes are generally moderately priced. The material may seem difficult to some, but generally these classes may be taken again and again. Often there are intensive review classes that meet the day before the statewide tests.

You have little to fear. You don't have to be a math wizard or a highly creative writer to do well on the state test—or as an agent. Just about all you will ever have to write is an advertisement for your new listing or for an open house. You are usually permitted to use a calculator during the test. You can take the test repeatedly just as law students can take the bar exam again and again until they pass.

Stick with It

How far you go really is up to you. You must get training and you must be determined to be

The classes required to get a real estate license are usually moderately priced, and you can take the test over and over if you need to.

successful. You must work hard at the job and stay with it when things are slow, handle long and inconvenient working hours, and build your own future. If you take advantage of the great potential and opportunities, you can make great things happen for yourself in real estate.

Start preparing now. The sooner you begin your pursuit, the easier it's going to be. Read on. You're about to sail into a great career with an exciting number of related areas also open to you.

2

Pre-Licensing Activities

What if you know that real estate is definitely for you, but you aren't able to enter the business at this particular time in your life? Maybe you are still in school and aren't old enough to take the classes. Maybe you can't fit the classes into your work schedule for several months. Maybe you have to deal with some other obligations before you can actually get into the real estate business.

Perhaps you've also realized that it will take a while for the commission checks to start coming to you. You have called or written to your state's real estate commission and understand that you will need some additional education. You have already pretty much figured out which class schedule would best fit your lifestyle when you are ready—but is there anything you could be doing in the meantime that would make you more knowledgeable, more marketable as an agent?

By all means! It is understood that you will soon take the classes, pass the state test, and join a brokerage. Though most agents don't even think

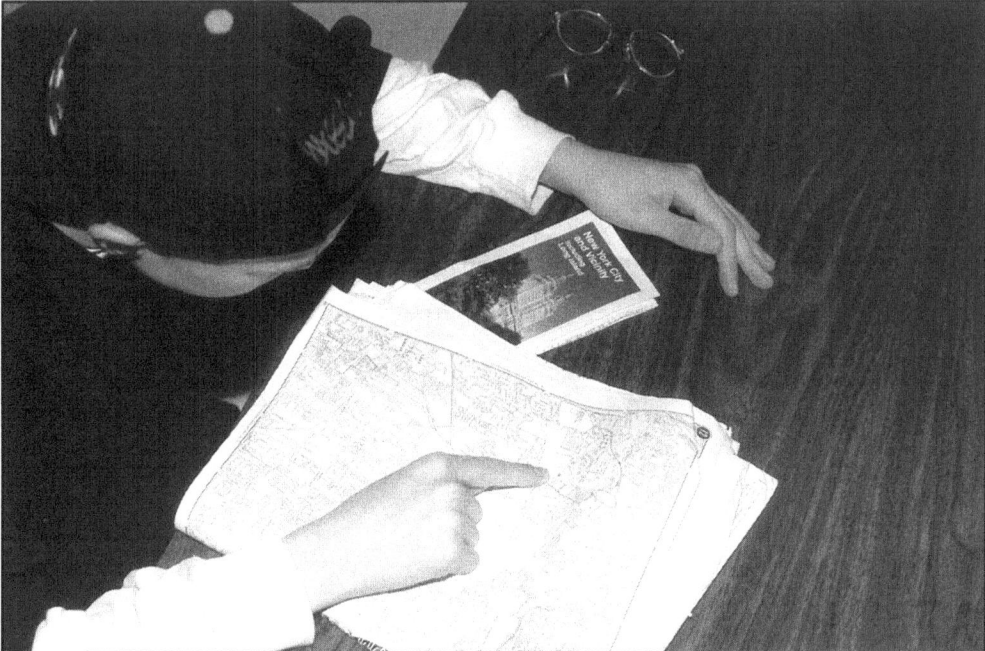

Studying maps of the area you expect to be working in can help you prepare for a career as a real estate agent.

about pre-licensing activities, these activities can be extremely helpful. Pre-licensing activities can give you a better background than some veteran agents will have after years of experience.

Prepare Yourself

Whether it will be six months or two years before you can realistically become a real estate agent, you will be amazed at how much preparation you can do on your own. Individualized self-study will help make that first day at the office in your chosen field less frightening.

Know Your Surroundings

One such activity is simply to study maps of the area where you expect to be working. If it is a large city, this task can be fairly difficult. You need to know the location of virtually every street. You wouldn't want to get lost trying to find a short avenue nestled between two small streets. And you certainly don't want a client getting lost because you couldn't give accurate directions to a location.

If you will be working in a small town, you should also get to know all the outlying areas. Take note of various routes, and figure out the best ways to get from one town to another, including using country roads. Knowing some history about these nearby communities is a nice added touch.

Learning About Homes

You might also want to look at some books on home styles. Some agents can easily identify a ranch house or a Cape Cod house but are unsure of whether a certain house is a cottage or a bungalow. Why not have some of this knowledge even before licensing?

House Plans

Invest in (or borrow from the library) a $5 to $20 book of house plans. Such a book or magazine can tell you about the different styles of homes, floor plans, how to figure square footage, dollars per square foot needed to build extra features, and a host of other factors that enter into the pricing of a home.

All this means that one day when an agent has a new listing with "a split-bedroom floor plan, located on Route 410 at the first intersection past

You can find books of floor plans at your local public library.

Greenleaf turnoff," you may know exactly where it is located and what kind of house that is. You may even have seen the house, especially if you have made it your business to understand routes, roads, and locations. (All that and you don't even have a license yet!)

Listing Sheets

Why not get familiar with listing sheets? You can also learn a lot about the business by borrowing a listing book or a stack of past listing sheets from a real estate office. These sheets include a great deal of data on each house—square footage, basement, age of roof, etc.

Taxes and Assessment

You could also visit the tax office. Look at property tax papers. Learn why some houses that have the same square footage are taxed differently from each other. Understand exemptions. Does family income or age have any effect on taxing? Talk to the clerk and have him or her explain exemptions, sheriff's sales, etc. Only a small portion of this information will be covered in the real estate classes, so you must learn it either on the job or on your own.

Visit the assessor's office to see why a house is valued as it is. Does a brick home get assessed higher than a similar frame home with the same square footage? Why? Do you get a higher assessment because you added a room or a garage? Why?

The clerk at a tax office can explain property tax exemptions.

You might even want to visit your local zoning office. You will understand the need to be correct when you talk about zoning laws with your clients. There are some areas with special covenants (agreements) regarding the rules for building certain types of structures on a property. A subdivision map is a good introduction to such special situations. Some subdivisions don't permit travel trailers, buses, or semitrailers to be parked on the street. You can't know every rule, but like a lawyer, you will know where to go to find the information.

Take a look at a plat book. Unless you were raised on a farm, you may be surprised to see how a piece of farm ground is detailed in a plat book. A plat book will show you, for instance, which roads run by the farm, how far back the land extends, and who the owner is. Think of how great you'll

Most parents are concerned about where their children will attend school, so it is important for a real estate agent to have information about local school districts.

sound when you have an interview with the owner of a respected, money-making real estate firm.

Don't forget about school districts. Know how to determine where a child will go to school if you sell a family a certain home. This is vital information that all parents will want to know. Even more stressful to some parents might be where their children can play sports and hang out after school and on weekends. Such details are important to your client. You want to know where such information is found, and you want to be able to find out in a matter of a few minutes. This makes you look prepared and capable. Besides, it's comforting to know that you are beginning to learn the business even before you start taking the classes.

Such pre-licensing activities can only put you ahead of the game. Knowing where subdivisions are, what new industries are moving into the area, which school districts are where, how zoning works, and a lot more about your area will help make you the kind of agent every potential buyer and seller wants to know.

3

Finding the Right Broker

Are there other steps to take after you have made the commitment to enter the field of real estate? Most definitely yes. There is at least one more critical issue: finding the right broker.

Meeting with Brokers

Someday in the not-too-distant future, you will sit down and talk to a person who will interview you for a position with a real estate firm. This person will discuss the real estate field with you and then possibly welcome you to his or her company. The question is, should that meeting take place before or after you have your license? When should you start thinking about your future mentor, your associate, your leader? Why not meet the broker before you have your license?

Such a meeting usually starts with a telephone call or a well-written letter. If you choose to write a letter, have someone proofread it for you. Have as many people as possible read it over to make

It is important to be polite and have a positive attitude when you meet with a potential employer.

sure you are saying exactly what you want to say, clearly and respectfully.

During the Interview

You should, of course, explain that you are pursuing a career in real estate. You can add that you are enrolled in classes at the present time or that you are scheduled to start on a certain day (or, perhaps, that you are looking into enrollment for the future). Be honest. Brokers don't want to hire liars. A firm's reputation is one of its most valuable assets, and brokers are very careful when selecting new agents. Make sure that you present yourself in the best possible light.

Most brokers will probably understand your situation, and chances are they will be impressed by your ambition, especially if you mention some of your pre-licensing experience. After all, everyone starts out as a beginner. The fair-minded broker will recognize your courage and determination and will most likely admire that character trait in a beginner. In any case, be presentable. You don't have to be a style-setter. Just be neat and polite and try to show a positive attitude, a willingness to work hard, and a determination to succeed.

Think about it. If a company, or agency, decides to hire you, it will be taking a real chance on you, a real risk. The agency is usually willing to provide you with a suitable workplace, your own desk and chair, a telephone, some company literature, and the use of the secretarial staff to take messages. You will probably have access to a computer, printer, and fax machine. All of these items cost the agency a sizable amount of money. You have to make a reasonably good impression or the broker will not take the chance, and you may have to settle for a lesser company.

On an interview like this, when you haven't even completed the necessary real estate courses, the best approach is to be truthful. Sometimes just being a sincere, honest person can be enough to win over an employer. At the very least, you will gain experience in interviewing and will see how a real estate company operates. You can even ask about the possibility of reinterviewing with the company when you have taken the required courses.

What to Look for in an Employer

Finding the best broker to work for is tremendously important. As a rule, most companies pay their agents nothing up front, even to help new agents get started. Of course, it's always possible that you will have made such a good impression during the interview that the owner will be willing to loan you part of the money needed for your classes, but this is a long shot. You may also be eligible for some school grants or loans. Ask your broker for information about such grants, or do some research in the library or on-line.

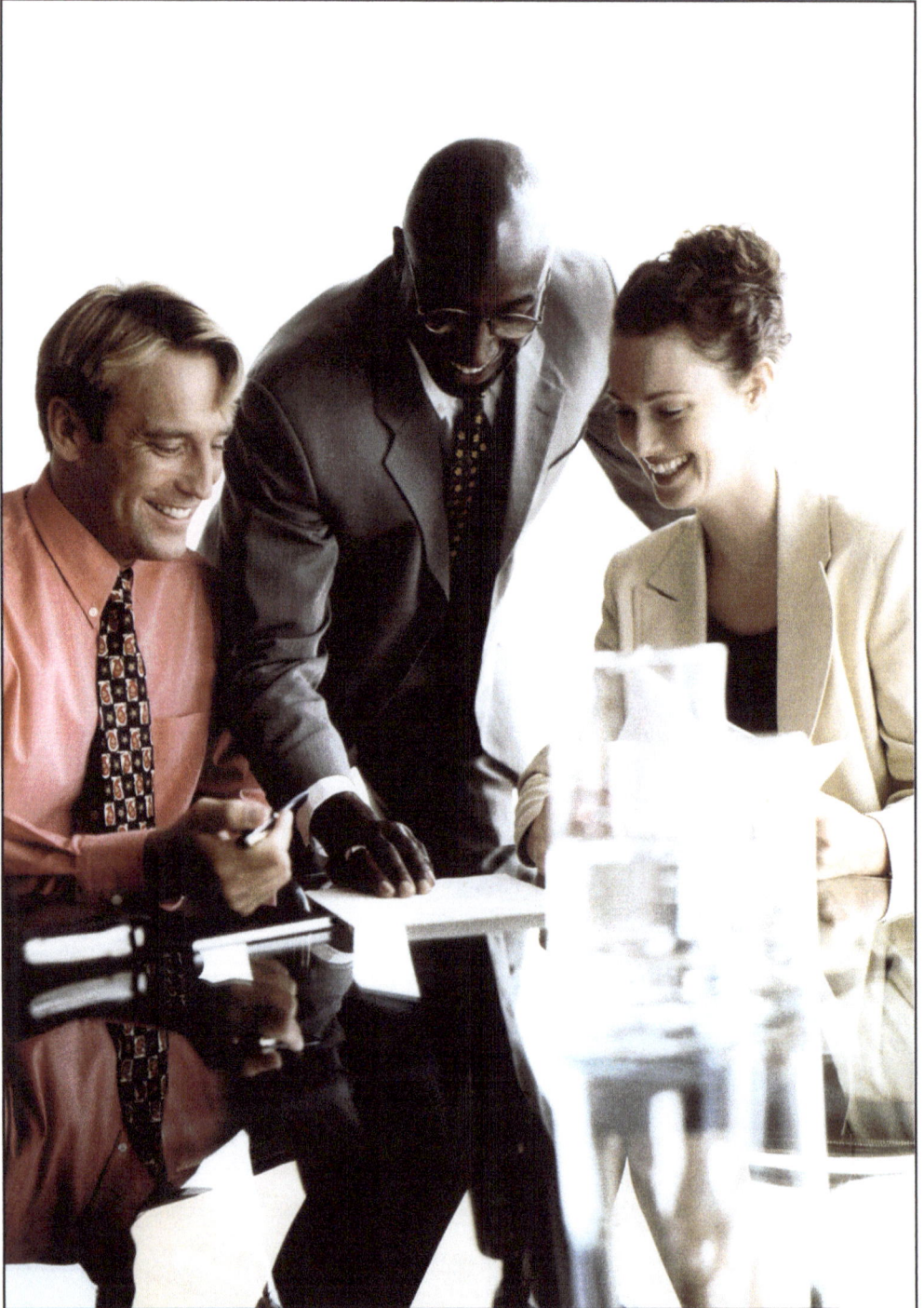
A company that provides on-the-job training is an ideal workplace for a novice real estate agent.

Training

Working for a pleasant broker is one thing, but just as important to a new agent is working for a company that provides thorough on-the-job training. There is so much more to learn about the real estate field than what the classes cover. These courses are primarily designed to help you understand the laws that govern your state. They explain specific legal issues such as housing terms, real estate laws, the taxing of property, and water rights. All of that is important, but what you want at this stage is in-depth training.

What a new agent needs from the broker at first is one-on-one or small class sessions to demonstrate how to handle various situations. For example, how do you go about finding listings or buyers? What's the best way to negotiate a sale if one of your parties, the buyer or seller, is upset about something? When do you use an abstract and when do you use title insurance? When do you go with your client to the bank to apply for a loan? How do you know which bank is most likely to finance your client? Does the child's playset in the yard stay with the property? What if the property has termites or a bad water system? The questions are endless.

Clearly, before you go out on your first listing, you want to be fully trained. Don't settle for less. You don't want to go out on your first appointment and find out that you are not adequately prepared. Look for a company that offers opportunities for on-the-job training. Many people in your position don't bother to meet the broker before accepting a

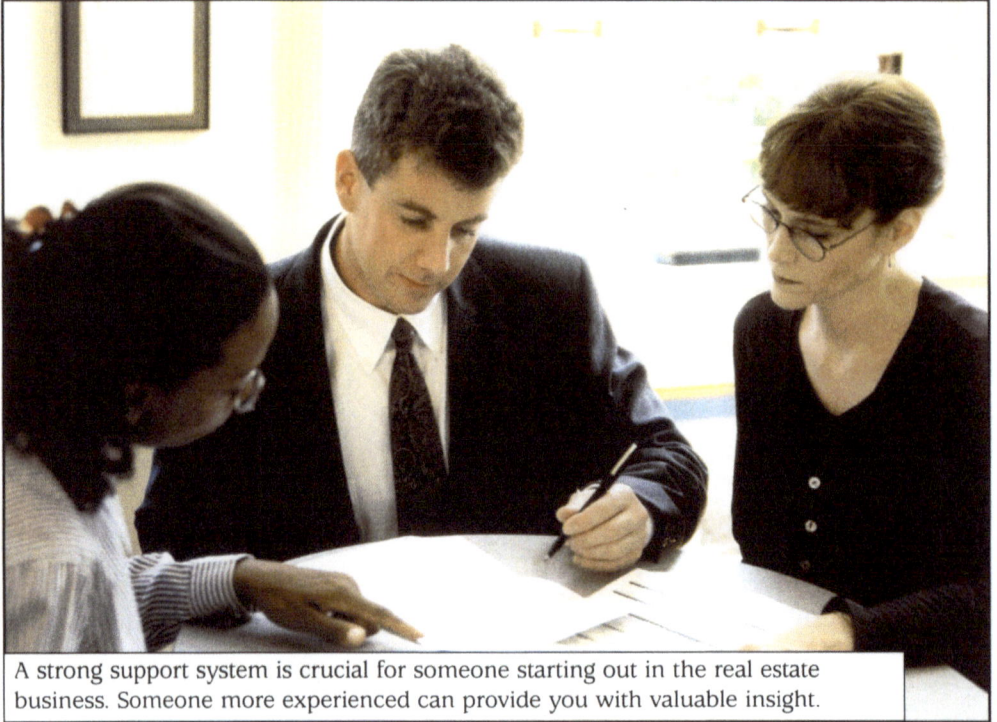

A strong support system is crucial for someone starting out in the real estate business. Someone more experienced can provide you with valuable insight.

job, yet doing so is one of the best investments of time and energy you can make.

Support

In the beginning, you will need and want a strong support system. It's important to know that there will be someone around to help you understand a legal complication when an issue arises. You will want to know that someone will be there to talk to when a really big transaction comes along and you don't feel comfortable handling it alone.

You'll more than likely be somewhat timid about a lot of things, such as amending a purchase agreement, negotiating a sale, understanding a certain mortgage company's fees, and loan origination points. That first closing at a bank can be especially frightening.

28

Good in-house training covers these kinds of situations. In time, as you confront some of these situations and hear how others went about solving similar problems, you will become increasingly knowledgeable and confident in your ability to deal with a variety of situations.

Even so, after several years in the business, even veteran agents appreciate having someone to whom they can turn. They often like to "run something by the broker." You really never outgrow your need for the right broker, good training, and a strong support system.

Asking Around

To get a better idea of what a company is like, talk with some of the agents. Do they seem relatively happy with the company? Are the literature bins filled with materials that make their job easier? Is the equipment in the office fairly up-to-date? Are there enough computers for everyone to use? Does the firm have a Web page and access to the Internet? Don't be afraid to ask questions. These are things that you need to know up-front.

If the broker doesn't encourage you to visit the other agents, just look around the office. Hopefully you will be given an office tour. Arrive at the office early on the day of your interview to get a feel for the place. You will see that agents come in all sizes, shapes, and ages. They will probably vary greatly in terms of dress, personality, experience, and selling techniques. Do the agents at this company seem to get along

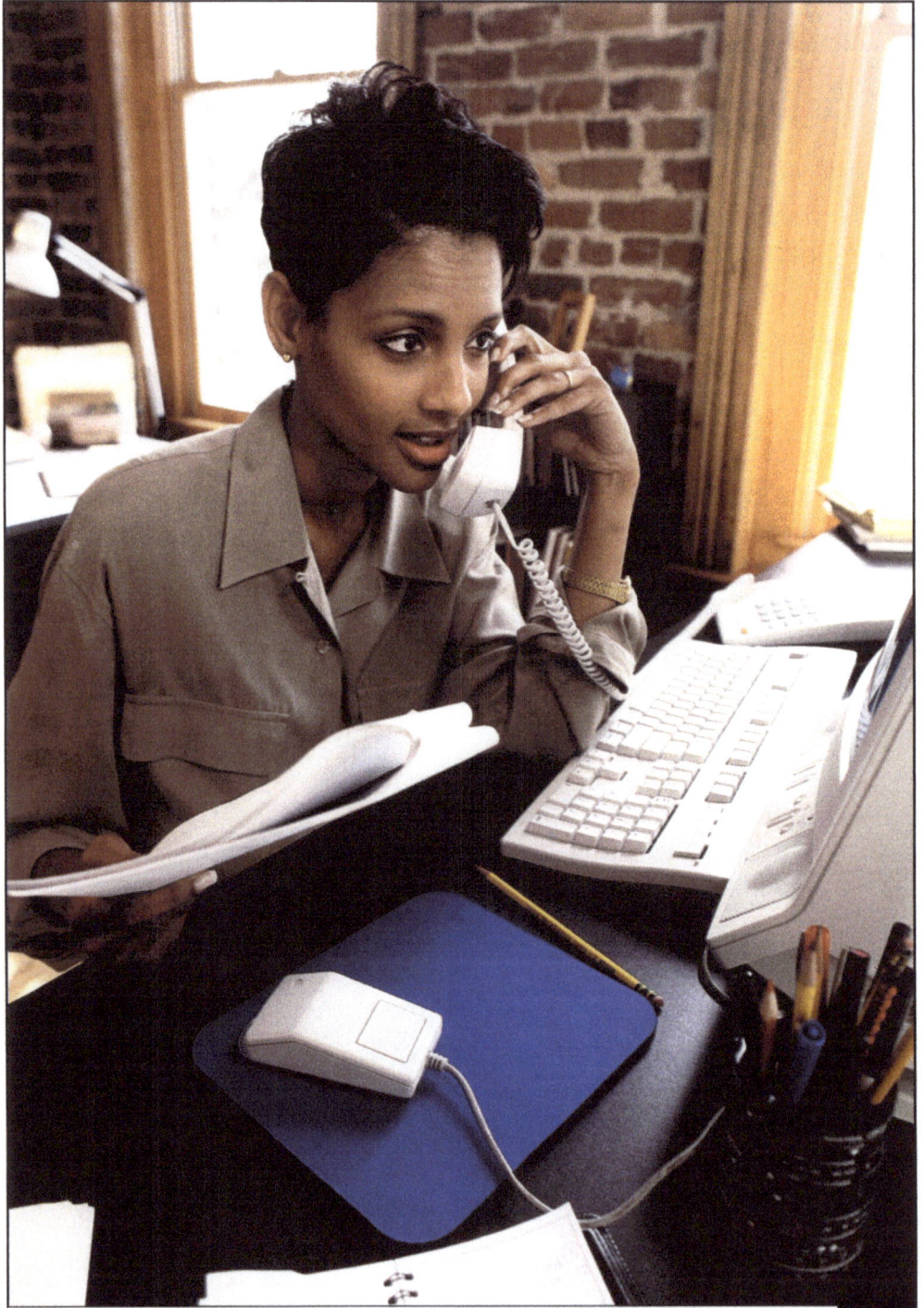

Unless you have prior sales experience, you may need to develop phone skills for your career as a real estate agent.

with each other? Can you see yourself working in that environment?

What Will I Be Learning?

Although it may seem silly now, unless you have some prior sales experience, you will probably have to learn how to communicate effectively on the phone. You don't want to lose a customer just because you didn't seem serious enough or were afraid to ask key questions.

It also will be important to know how to attract new prospects or clients. How do you market properties? How many hours per week will you be given floor time—time in which you are the agent designated to receive incoming calls from potential clients? Many agents no longer need telephone time. They have generated enough business on their own and are too busy to take on more clients at the moment. They may, in fact, have someone working for them, running errands such as picking up abstracts, calling owners for an appointment, or doing an open house. Until you are that busy, you will want that floor time. How often are you entitled to it? How does the agency attract clients?

Again, the number one asset for any agent, young or old, student or retiree, is personal training. Don't settle for less. Keep making appointments with brokers until you are satisfied with what you see. Remember, if a broker doesn't have time now to talk to you as an interested (though unlicensed) agent, chances are he or she won't have time for you later on.

Don't Give Up!

This may all seem overwhelming, but making a career choice is one of the biggest decisions of your life. Make it based on knowledge. If real estate sounds like the right profession for you, and you are willing to learn and to work hard at your career, you can do it and you can do it well. What's more, you may become a top-notch agent making a very comfortable living. The sky is the limit in real estate.

Personal satisfaction in your work, your ability to make a good living, and your independence while doing something you truly enjoy will be well worth all the planning and hard work that made it possible.

4

Responsibilities and Duties

From what you have read and learned, it should be clear that there are many challenges to making a living as a real estate agent. As is true of most careers, being successful in the real estate field requires hard work and dedication. Ideally, this hard work will lead not only to financial success but also to personal satisfaction. With lots of planning and a little bit of luck, you will be able to say that you truly enjoy your work: the freedom, the variety, and the opportunity to help match people with the homes that are best for them.

Above all, to do well, be respected, and develop a list of clients who come back to you time and time again for your knowledge and expertise, you must have a good understanding of, and a strong dedication to, your duties and responsibilities. You must know what is expected of you and do it so well that your clients feel 100 percent confident in your abilities.

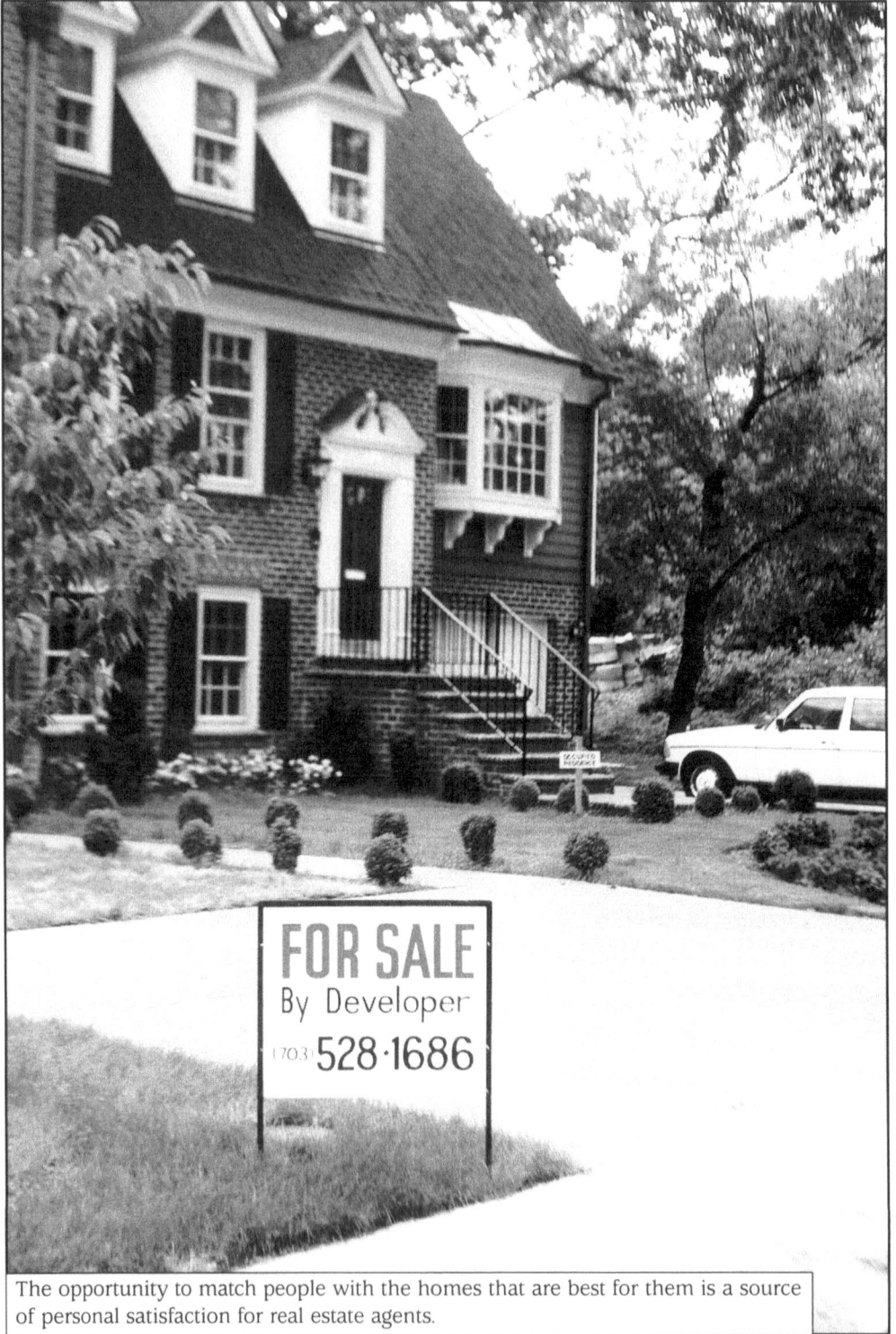

The opportunity to match people with the homes that are best for them is a source of personal satisfaction for real estate agents.

Meeting Changing Needs

Everybody needs a place to call home, to store personal belongings, to sleep—a place of their own. But what people want and need in a home can vary enormously, depending on their financial situation, the size of their family, their space requirements, their personal taste, and many other factors.

The same is true of people who are selling a piece of property. Each has a different set of circumstances and reasons for putting the property on the market. Sellers need help as well.

Fortunately for the agent, both buyers' and sellers' needs keep changing—often within a few short months or years—and this important "repeat business" is going to be a crucial part of your personal success. Your base of clients will gradually grow as your returning clients recommend you to more people and as you widen your center of influence.

Keeping Track

It is crucial to develop a system for storing information about each of your clients, especially as your base of clients begins to grow. At first you may simply have a loose-leaf notebook, three-by-five-inch file cards with information about each customer, or perhaps an electronic organizer. Later you will probably have to depend on a computer database to handle your needs.

A good personal database can help you keep track of clients and sellers.

A good personal database is the key to building your own business. Every time you add new clients and sellers or update information about them, you are increasing the chances that you will eventually find a property that suits your clients' needs and, more important, that they are happy with.

How do you find out about a client's needs? A good agent will sit down with new clients to discuss their preferences, what they can afford, and any specific requests that they may have. Then you can begin to look together for homes within this price range that best suit their needs.

When looking for property for Client A, you may find that you have located the perfect home for Client B. A growing inventory of buyers and sellers will give you an opportunity to make a very good living.

You keep track of Clients A, B, C—what they have and have not liked, how their needs have changed—until you find a successful match. You keep in touch with them as often as it takes. Let them know when you have found a place that looks promising. If you haven't found anything, tell them that as well. They must never feel that you have forgotten about them or let them down.

Keeping track of all of this information is a lot of work. Agents in the business are the first to admit that there is a lot of organization needed and lots of legwork before you get a paycheck. There is also a lot of disappointment, both on your part and on the part of the client, when the pieces do not fit. The family becomes discouraged and you don't get paid.

This is where the database comes in. Maybe next year the client will have more money to spend. For now you may be able only to point out options, but you still have their name, and they have yours.

Building Trust

Your buyers have come to you for assistance in a very important matter. They are placing their trust in you to make sure that the property they buy is within their price range, that they are getting their money's worth, and that you will be honest in your dealings with them. The sellers that you work with want to know that you have assessed their property accurately and are suggesting a fair price range. Both buyers and sellers want a successful, happy closing.

For a real estate agent, it is great that so many people need help in the serious business of finding a home. They want to find their "castle" without driving up and down every street and country road. They will appreciate an agent with up-to-date information on all the available properties in an area, including price, number and size of bedrooms, location, financing options, home inspections, lot size, and more. They will be happy to find a hard-working, patient, enthusiastic agent to work with them, and they will expect you to be as willing and anxious as they are about finding the perfect place.

If a perfect match doesn't happen immediately, your buyers want to know that you, their agent, will be watching the market daily and will keep them updated.

Listen Up!

Getting off to a good start with your client is important. You want to develop a strong rapport, a warm relationship, with this new client. Being a good listener is one of the best ways an agent can develop this rapport. Your new clients want and need for you to listen carefully. They are about to make a major purchase.

You should take notes and ask questions, and the clients will eagerly tell you about their needs and wants. Let them talk. You can gain valuable information and save precious time by paying attention.

As you work with more and more people and observe successful agents at work, you will notice

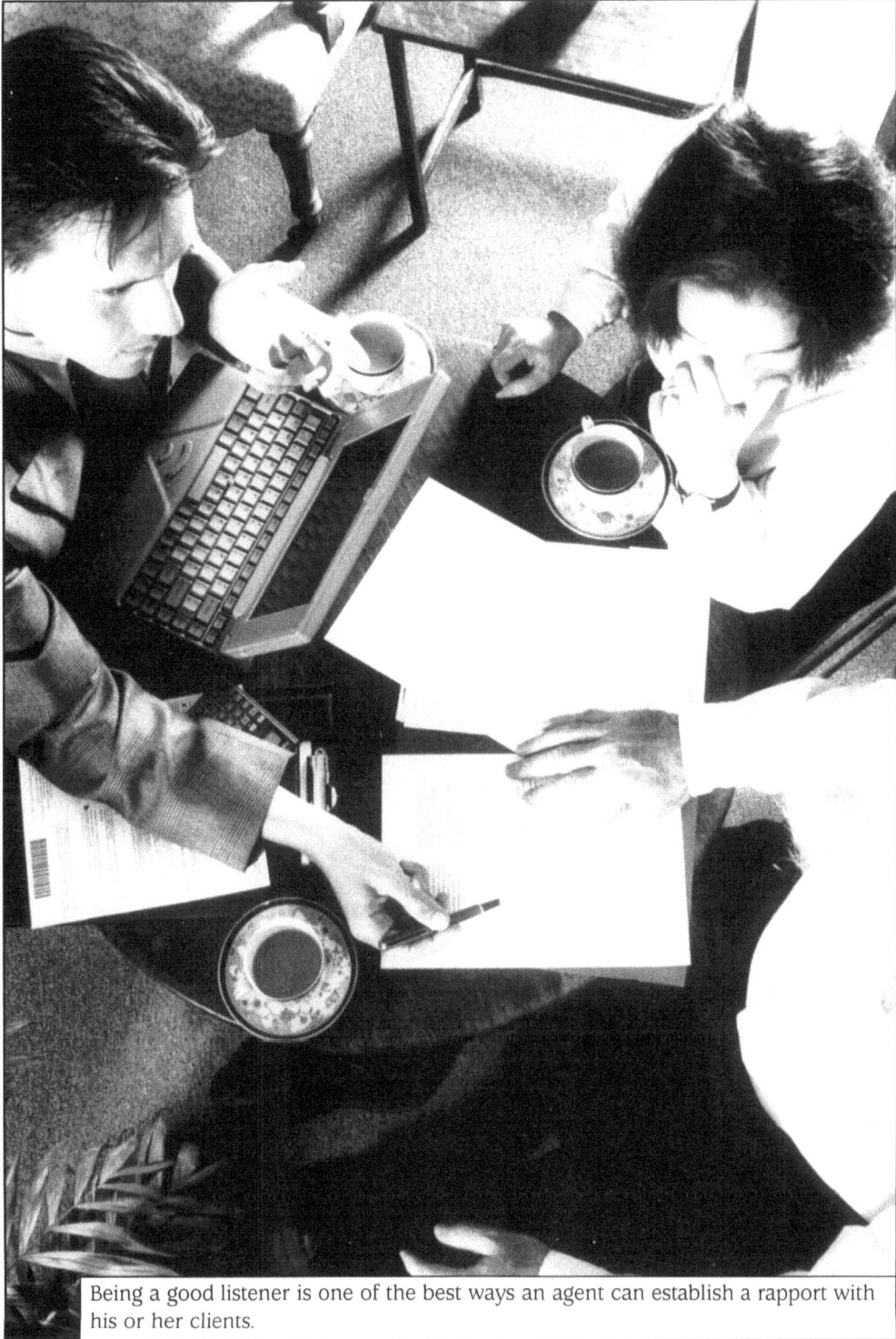
Being a good listener is one of the best ways an agent can establish a rapport with his or her clients.

how careful they are to get off to a good start with every client. That's because they know that trust will grow when the seeds are planted right away.

Knowing about market and financing options in detail will also help you establish strong relationships. Clients will have questions about financing, monthly payments, and down payments. They must feel good about putting their situation into the hands of a stranger.

Starting the Search

Once you have a clear idea of your client's needs and price range, you are ready to begin the search. You will check all available sources to help you locate suitable homes and work with this information. Every office will have some kind of system for you to follow.

Usually most properties will be listed in a computer database. Information provided will include photos as well as information about various aspects of the property, including price, lot size, possession, and condition. Agents use this system, plus their own knowledge and experience, to begin making matches between clients and available homes. You will set up appointments with homeowners and begin showing your buyers the homes that seem to fit their needs.

Finding Listings

All sales start with getting a listing. If a family has asked you to handle a property, the first steps are

Getting a listing and putting up a sign are among the first steps to selling a home.

to put up a sign and get the property on the market and into the computer database for everyone to see. In this case you are the listing agent, also known as the seller's agent. If the new listing is posted by someone else in the office or from a neighboring office, you become a buyer's agent. You will be working primarily for the buyer.

Getting or hearing about a new listing is great news. It may be just what you and Client D have been trying to find. It sounds like a wonderful house, and you want your client to see it before another family buys it.

Budgeting Your Time

New agents won't always know the answers to every client's questions, but a strong office support system, including a willing broker, is the key to getting these answers quickly. The new agent will check into the problems and questions immediately.

Real estate agents are as busy as they want to be. Follow-up takes time, as does searching for and showing properties, interviewing clients, making telephone calls, and doing research. And when these things aren't keeping you too busy, there's always work to be done—attracting new clients, studying bank rates, and entering information into the computer database.

In addition, it is a good idea to plan on seeing some vacant houses so that when you show them to buyers, you will be prepared to say, "Yes, I can

Many agents preview a property before showing it. The more knowledge an agent has of a home, the easier it is to sell.

show you that home. As a matter of fact, I've been there. It was renovated about a year ago, it has a small loft that would make a nice study or library, and there are lots of shelves in the basement for storage, a work bench, or a home gym." You can sell anything better if you know what you are selling.

Some agents preview each home before showing it. This helps them know all about the property ahead of time. Many companies make it a practice to tour every home that was listed by any of the agents in their office the prior week.

The best way to figure out how to handle your schedule is to watch other successful brokers at work. Pay attention to where they devote their time and what their priorities are. You can even ask them if they have any shortcuts to recommend.

Pros and Cons of Being an Agent

As with any career, there are pros and cons—good parts and bad parts—about being a real estate agent. Read on to get a better sense of the advantages and disadvantages of this job.

Cons

The responsibilities and duties of an agent may seem overwhelming. You must not only sell the property, which means that you actually write an offer and the owner accepts it, but you must also help your buyer through the many steps on the

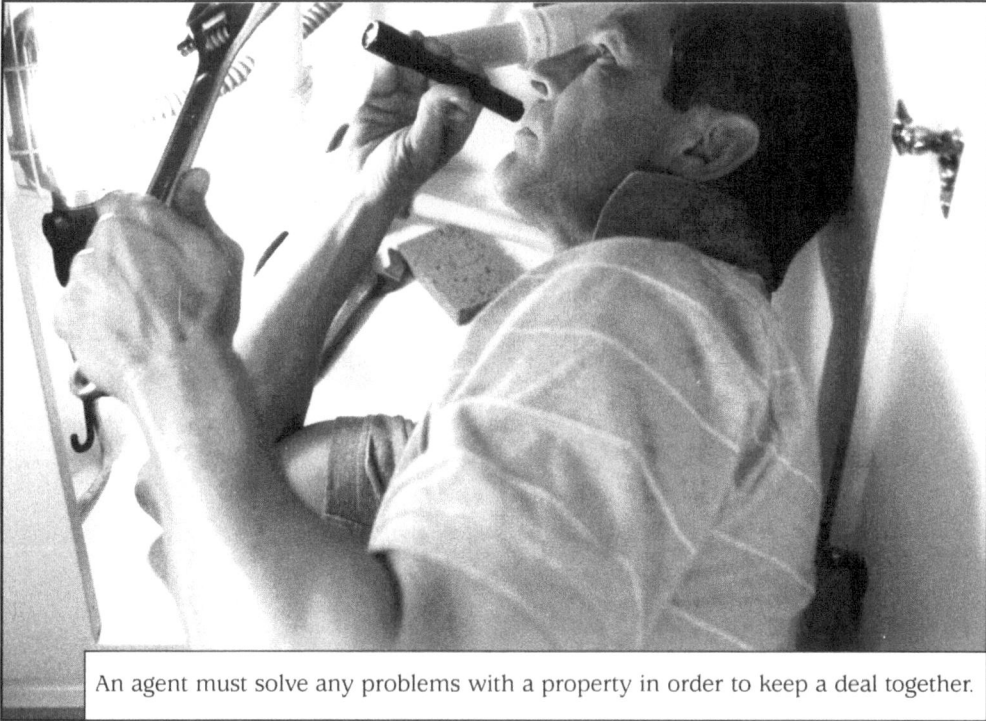

An agent must solve any problems with a property in order to keep a deal together.

way to closing. You must be concerned with getting your people to the bank, waiting for the bank's appraisal of the house, receiving the credit report on your buyer, and seeing that the client has home inspections and homeowner's insurance.

As an agent, you will get the abstract or other necessary documents to their proper place: the title company, attorney, abstractor, or wherever they should go. You will discuss the home inspection report and help the buyer decide what repairs should be made in order to go ahead with the purchase. You will study the disclosure papers if your state has disclosure laws and be ready to point out claims made on the form.

If there is a termite problem, a wet basement, a poorly functioning furnace, storm damage, or any such problem, you, as the agent, will come to the rescue with your expertise. You won't actually mop up the basement or fix the furnace, but you will support your client through these crises in any legal way possible. You will try to keep the deal together and solve the problems that arise for your client and yourself.

Aside from the many duties that the real estate agent must take on, another major downside to the job is frequent disappointment. Not every sale is going to go through. You will not be able to list or sell every home that you find. You must learn to handle rejection. It's going to happen and it's painful. You have to be strong and determined.

Pros

Still, the real estate business is exciting. It doesn't take a great amount of money for training, yet your income can match that of other professionals who have spent several years in college or an apprenticeship program. The work is varied, so no day is the same. You are not tied down to a desk for a major portion of your life. You are not on an assembly line in a factory. You come and go as you like.

If your child is ill at school, you can leave immediately without punching a time clock. A secretary will take messages and usually another agent will cover for you while you are out of reach. If you need to take a trip, you can usually have a colleague cover for you. All that is required is some planning.

If you like independence, freedom to plan your own schedule, and the idea of working with people and matching people and properties together, you will enjoy being in real estate. If you are willing to work hard, learn, listen, get organized, and be patient, you can become a top-notch agent.

If you think that this kind of career sounds right for you, there is no reason to wait. You're never too young to get on board. If you are older and seeking a career change, age need not stand in your way. Many fine agents are still working (and doing very well) in their seventies.

Find out what your state requires for licensing, take the short courses, and pass the state test. Contact the broker of your choice, and with a determined, positive attitude, you can go further than you ever thought possible. It's your life and your decision.

5

Related Careers

What if you think you are interested in a real estate career but don't think that you would be comfortable in selling, at least not right now? What if you would prefer regular hours and a regular paycheck?

If it is selling that makes you nervous, there are careers within the field that can open the door to sales or simply offer you non-selling opportunities. Similarly, there are jobs that offer regular hours and pay. Some of these jobs require getting a real estate license, whereas others do not.

Since states differ as to which positions require a license, it is best to check with your state's licensing agency or real estate commission. You can find much of this information by contacting the sources listed at the back of this book.

The following are some careers related to real estate that might interest you.

An apartment manager handles the renting and upkeep of an apartment complex.

Apartment Manager

An apartment manager handles the renting and upkeep of an apartment complex. With the growth of apartments, condos, office buildings, and, now more than ever, senior housing and subsidized low income complexes, this is an area with lots of opportunity for growth.

The position requires some office work, as well as documenting income, writing ads, inspecting units, and showing clients what is available. It may also require taking deposits, explaining contracts, getting credit reports, calling in a carpet cleaner, ordering new curtains, and certainly, calling the maintenance person the moment an air conditioner doesn't work. In most states, a license is required to be an apartment manager.

Appraiser

Appraisers have completed additional course work and are qualified, and hired, to place a value on a piece of property. This usually involves a detailed report that often includes photos of the property, comparisons to other properties, proper zoning, an assessment of positive and negative features, and other important information about the property.

Bookkeeper-Accountant

The bookkeeper-accountant is responsible for such tasks as tracking financial records, paying bills and

Appraisers are hired to place a value on a piece of property.

commissions, handling payroll, and making sure that all financial forms required by law are filled out properly. Certification for this position often requires a degree from a two- or four-year college.

Broker

Brokers are licensed real estate agents who have taken advanced courses that allow them to open a real estate office and have others working with their firm.

Closing Agent

A closing agent conducts the meeting where the actual change of ownership takes place. This meeting, called a closing, is done at a bank, lending institution, attorney's office, or any other place agreed upon by all parties.

Courier

A courier is an employee whose duty is to run errands for a real estate company. Duties may include picking up and delivering documents, putting up and taking down real estate signs, and shopping for supplies.

Home Inspector

Home inspectors are hired, usually by the buyer, to carefully check a house for physical and mechanical defects before the property changes hands. The inspector often hires others, usually called apprentices, to assist him or her. This opens up another job for an interested person.

Maintenance Engineer

Maintenance engineers keep a company's buildings in good physical condition by repairing plumbing, wiring, air conditioning, and other systems.

Office Manager

An office manager reports directly to the principal broker, assisting him or her with a number of executive tasks. Office managers are often responsible for operating a branch office.

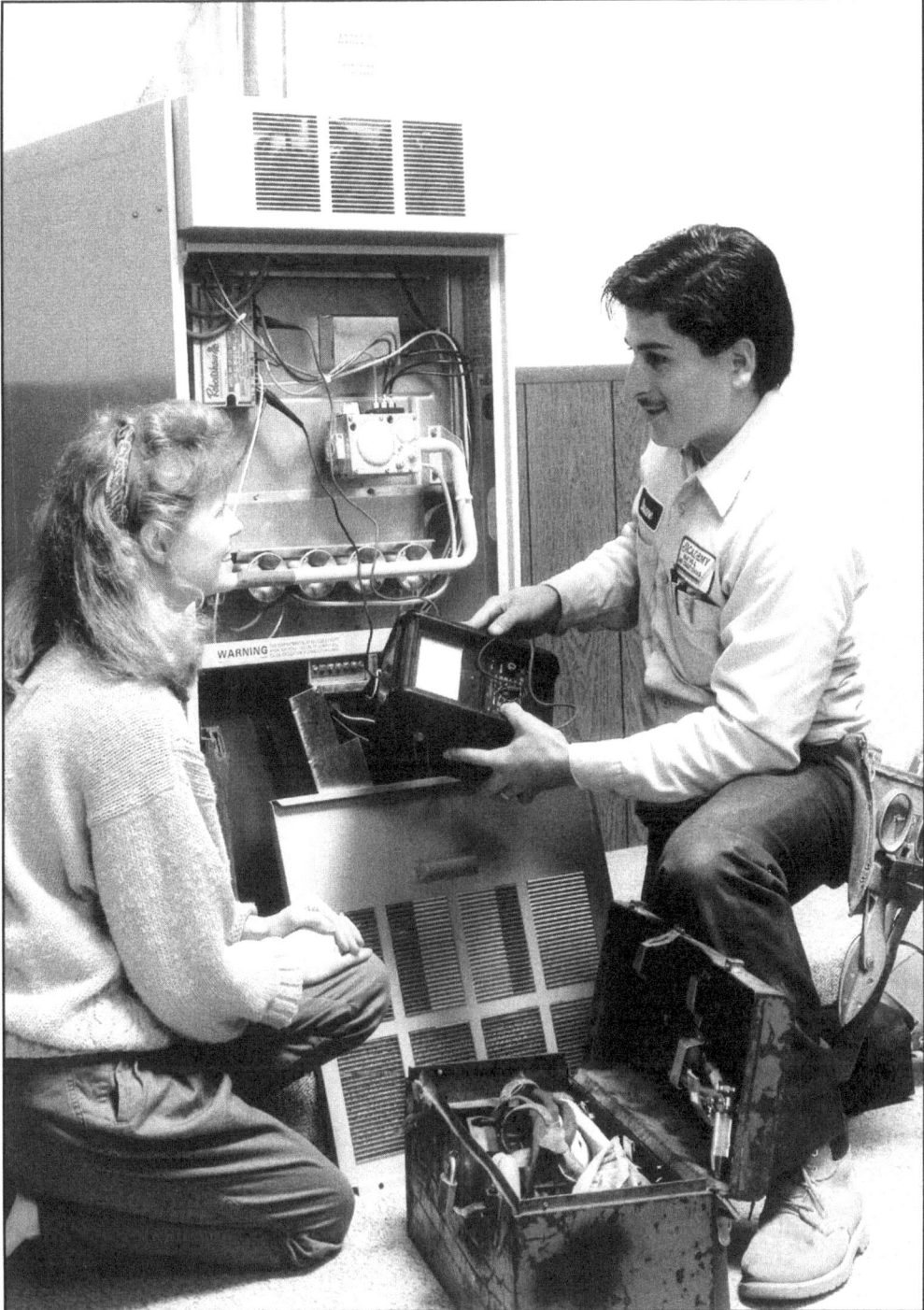

A maintenance engineer's job is to keep a building in good physical condition.

Professional Assistant

A professional assistant is an executive secretary who works under the direction of an agent who doesn't have time to handle office paperwork.

Receptionist

A receptionist is a secretary who sits at the front desk and whose duties include answering the telephone, greeting clients, scheduling meetings with new clients, signing out keys, and accommodating walk-in clients.

Relocation Agent

Relocation agents act as both secretaries and agents, handling incoming and outgoing referrals and the properties that are assigned to their firm by a relocation company.

Rental Agent

Rental agents are responsible for collecting rents, showing units, and keeping the properties in suitable condition.

Technician

Technicians are in charge of keeping computers, fax machines, and other electronic equipment in proper working order.

Title Searcher

A title searcher is a clerk or owner of an abstract or title company who works on bringing the history of the property, called the abstract, up-to-date. This person must have the ability to proofread accurately and to research courthouse records and other documentation to track down important information.

Where to Go from Here

These are but a sampling of jobs that are available in real estate offices. Think about your particular interests, needs, and plans for the future. You should realize that, as a young person, if you go into sales you may have to live at home a little longer than you may have planned. It usually takes several months before you begin to earn enough money to pay for a car, a professional wardrobe, and even an expensive briefcase. Beepers and cellular phones will follow.

If you know that a career in real estate is really what you want, now is the time to start making it happen. Perhaps you want to buy houses, fix them up, and own some rentals.

The important thing to remember for now is to budget your time and money well and to remain patient. The possibilities for success and satisfaction are endless.

Glossary

abstract A document that indicates how many times, when, and to whom a property has been sold. This document also details the history of the property, explaining when it was divided into smaller parcels of land, such as during the development of subdivisions.

agent The salesperson or representative of a real estate company. He or she works with a client to buy or sell a piece of property.

broker An agent licensed to operate a real estate office on his or her own.

client The buyer or seller whom the real estate agent represents.

closing The point or place at which the property actually changes hands, when all parties agree on the sale.

commission   Payment made to the agency and agents in exchange for real estate services. To the agent, it is the equivalent of a paycheck.

cons   Negative sides, or disadvantages, of a decision or issue.

exemptions   Factors that reduce the amount of taxes a person has to pay.

floor time   The time during which you are the agent designated to receive incoming calls from potential clients.

house plan   Diagram of a house, detailing its layout.

listing   A contract between the seller and the real estate agency.

plat book   Record book showing minute details of a property, including nearby roads, rivers running through the property, how far back the land extends, and who the owner is.

pre-licensing activities   Work done in the real estate field by a potential agent before he or she has received a license.

pros   Positive sides, or benefits, of a decision or issue.

school district   Area designated by the public school system to determine which children attend which public schools.

subdivision   Specifically designated area within a town, city, community, or county that has its own specific and unique realty laws.

title   Document pertaining to the legal ownership of a piece of property, building, or home.

title insurance   A policy taken out by the buyer that indicates that the property can be legally sold.

zoning laws   Laws that determine limitations on the types of buildings that can be constructed within different areas.

For More Information

In the United States

American Real Estate Society
Department of Finance—BU327E
James J. Nance College of Business
Cleveland State University
Cleveland, OH 44114
(216) 687-4732
Fax: (216) 687-9331
http://www.aresnet.org

IU Center for Real Estate Studies
Kelley School of Business
Indiana University
1309 East Tenth Street, Suite 738
Bloomington, IN 47405-1701
(812) 855-7794
Fax: (812) 855-9472
http://www.indiana.edu/ ~ cres

MIT Center for Real Estate
77 Massachusetts Avenue, W31–310
Cambridge, MA 02139-4307
(617) 253-4373
Fax: (617) 258-6991
http://web.mit.edu/cre/www

In Canada

British Columbia Real Estate Association (BCREA)
1155 West Pender Street, Suite 309
Vancouver, BC V6E 2P4
(604) 683-7702
Fax: (604) 683-8601
http://www.bcrea.bc.ca

Web Sites

Canadian Real Estate Association
http://www.mls.ca/mls/home.asp

Directory of United States and Canadian Real Estate
   Licensing Offices
http://recenter.tamu.edu/info/statelic.html

National Association of Realtors
http://www.realtor.com

Real Estate Research Institute
http://www.reri.org

For Further Reading

Hahn, Bruce W. *How to Sell Your Home Fast.* Arlington, VA: The American Homeowners Foundation Press, 1995.

Hodgkins, Lowell R. *How to Succeed as a Real Estate Salesperson.* Whitehall, VA: Betterway Publications, Inc., 1990.

Irwin, Robert. *Tips and Traps When Selling a Home.* New York: McGraw-Hill, 1997.

Lindemann, Bruce J., and Jack P. Friedman. *How to Prepare for Real Estate License Examinations.* New York: Barron's Educational Series, Inc., 1990.

Thomsett, Michael C. *The Complete Guide to Selling Your Home.* Homewood, IL: Dow Jones-Irwin, 1989.

Wachtel, John L. *How to Buy Land.* New York: Sterling Publications, 1982.

WPW

Index

A
abstract, 27, 31, 45, 55
advice, getting, 9
apartment manager, 50
appraiser, 50
assessment, 18

B
bank, 27, 28, 42, 45, 51
bookkeeper-accountant, 50–51
broker/brokerage, 14, 22–32,
    42, 44, 47, 51, 52
    interviewing with, 24–25, 29
    meeting with, 22–23, 27
buyer, 21, 27, 35, 36, 40, 42, 44,
    45, 52
buyer's agent, 42

C
classes, taking, 11, 14, 18, 21,
    24, 25, 27
closing, 28, 37, 44, 51
    agent, 51–52
commission, 51
    checks, 14
courier, 52

D
database, 35–36, 37, 40, 42

F
financing, 27, 38, 40
floor time, 31

H
homes/houses, 6, 16, 18, 21, 33,
    35, 36, 38, 40, 42, 52, 55
    inspections, 38, 45
    inspector, 52
    plans, 16–18
    pricing, 16
    styles of, 16

I
insurance
    homeowner's, 45
    title, 27

L
land, 6, 19
laws, 27, 51
    disclosure, 45
license, real estate, 6, 10, 11, 16,

18, 22, 47, 48
state test, 11, 14, 47
listing, 6, 11, 16, 27, 40, 42, 46
    agent, 42
    sheets, 18
loan, 27, 28
location, 16, 18, 38

M
maintenance engineer, 52
maps
    studying, 15–16
    subdivision, 19
market, 38, 40
mortgage company, 28

O
office manager, 52
open house, 11, 31
outlying areas, 16

P
people skills, 10
plat book, 19
pre-licensing activities, 14–21, 24
professional assistant, 54
property, 10, 19, 27, 31, 35, 36,
    37, 38, 40, 42, 44, 47, 50,
    52, 54, 55
    tax, 18, 27
purchase agreement, 28

R
real estate agent, 6, 11, 14, 15, 16,
    21, 27, 29, 31, 33, 36, 38,
    42, 44, 45, 46, 47, 51, 54
    pros and cons, 44–47

related careers, 48–55
responsibilities and duties
    of, 33–47
salary/pay, 6, 25, 32, 37, 46, 55
skills, 6, 9, 10
training for, 6, 11, 27–28,
    29, 31, 32, 46
receptionist, 54
relocation agent, 54
rental agent, 54

S
sales, 46
    experience, 31
    negotiating, 27, 28
school districts, 21
seller, 21, 27, 35, 36, 37, 42
seller's agent, 42
subdivision, 19, 21
    map, 19
support system, 28–29, 42

T
taxes, 18, 27
tax office, 18
technician, 54
title
    company, 55
    searcher, 55
trust, building, 37–38, 40

V
value, 6, 50

Z
zoning, 19, 21, 50
    office, 19

About the Author
Betty Clark lives and works in Indiana. She is the author of three children's books, including *Coping on a Tight Budget* for the Rosen Publishing Group.

Photo Credits
Cover and p. 53 © Ron Chapple/FPG International; pp. 2, 7, 36, 45 © Superstock; p. 10 © Brain T. Silak; p. 12 © Owen Franken/CORBIS; p. 15 by Kim Sonsky; p. 17 by Kitty Hsu; p. 19 by Ira Fox; p. 20 © Paul Conklin/Pictor; p. 23 © Anthony Nagelmann/FPG International; p. 26 © VCG/FPG International; p. 28 © Scott Barrow/International Stock; p. 30 © David Stover/Pictor; p. 34 © William Tucker/Pictor; p. 39 © Telegraph Colour Library/FPG International; p. 41 © Ping Amranand/Pictor; p. 43 © Annie Griffiths Belt/CORBIS; p. 49 © Robert Shafer/Pictor; p. 51 © Earl Kogler/International Stock.

Design
Geri Giordano

www.ingramcontent.com/pod-product-compliance
Lightning Source LLC
Chambersburg PA
CBHW042059210326
41597CB00045B/85